Lyrics for a Low Noon

Poems

by

James Ralston

Blue Light Press ❖ 1st World Publishing

1st WORLD
PUBLISHING

San Francisco ❖ Fairfield ❖ Delhi

LYRICS FOR A LOW NOON

1st World Library
PO Box 2211
Fairfield, IA 52556
www.1stworldpublishing.com

Blue Light Press
www.bluelightpress.com
bluelightpress@aol.com

Book & Cover Design
Melanie Gendron
melaniegendron999@gmail.com

Cover Art
Rosalind Brenner

Author Photo
Tim Snyder

First Edition

Library of Congress Control Number: 2018937464

ISBN 9781421838052

ACKNOWLEDGMENTS:

Versions of "Low Noon," "Power Lines" and "Last Tango Up Shit Creek" appeared in *The Sun: A Magazine of Ideas*; "Refrain," "Playing Time," "Jims," originally "Pegged" and "Love at Rest" appeared in the 2017 May/June issue of *The American Poetry Review*. "Then" and "The Year God and I Became One" appeared in the spring, 2018 *Solstice*.

I wish to thank the following persons:

the Frostburg Writing Group for its vigorous literary engagement since the mid-1980's, meeting twice monthly to critique works-in-progress. It has provided the workshop for ninety percent of the poems in this book;

Barbara Hurd, one of Group's original founders and for many years now its co-host, for her unflinching generosity and inspiration;

Stephen Dunn, the Group's other co-host, for raising the bar when he moved to Frostburg 16 years ago. A world class poet, he has also been a powerful teacher and a great friend. (Without him and Barbara, this book does not come to pass.);

Diane Frank and the editorial board of Blue Light Press for deciding that *Lyrics for a Low Noon* was worthy of publication; Rosalind Brenner for the terrific cover art; Tim Snyder for the author's photo, his zeal for "getting it right"; Melanie Gendron for so richly putting it all together;

other writer friends for the many pleasurable hours we spent exchanging and critiquing each other's work over the years: Jim Lithen, Jorn Bramann, Mike Grady, Chuck Collard, Keith Schlegel, Charles Sullivan, John Nevin, Bill Dudley, Karen Zealand, Jim Hadra, Doug Demars, C. J. Moll, Bryon MacWilliams, Matt Chelf, Michael Barbour;

and Sy Safransky (editor), Carol Ann Fitzgerald (managing editor), and Andrew Snee (senior editor) of *The Sun* for their longstanding encouragement and support. What a blessing it has been to be part of *The Sun*.

For my daughter, Holley;

for my son, Tyler, daughter-in-law, Mari,
and grandson, Andrew;

and for my friend, Jorn Bramann.

CONTENTS:

PART I: ECLIPSED

PART II: LOW NOON

PART III: PUTTING MY BODY TO BED

PART IV: LORD MAKE ME CHASTE, BUT NOT YET

PART I

ECLIPSED

LOVE AT REST

Love went down to wrestle death.
Now resting in the current,
love at best feels more like *like*.

A certain hue of pre-dawn light,
cobalt through an icy window,
I could say I somewhat like,

almost call out her name.
(Is this her bed I'm in or mine,
or am I sleeping in my van?)

Waking up from dead to numb,
from nothing much to shades of dawn,
I like not knowing where I am,

where time went, the short hand
from the long. I begin to roughly
comprehend certain esoteric films,

L'Eclisse, Mulholland Drive,
and feel the need to write again
aimless like-songs in my head.

THEN

Once I made love to a woman
with child. In my attic now, I find
a photo of her just starting to show,

she and her unborn shortly to die
in a motorcycle accident.
But how could I have known?

I was the life of the party then,
bouncing around, a cat who believed
in nine lives and always coming back.

And when she left the bar, I followed.
And when she came, she cried.
She was one of those who cry.

AMONG CARPENTER BEES

You don't sting me, I don't kill you.
We make a pact, and suddenly
this buzzing around my head

sounds like rain in the trees,
spring creeks running fast,
a hummingbird's wings.

Or those newlyweds next door
sawing boards, adding a room
onto their coffin, busy bees.

In my garden, morning glory
mingles in with poison ivy,
thistle, dog dung, hints of rot.

My cat enjoys a bird for lunch,
but I'm done with swatting things,
calling this a flower, that a weed,

culling out the right from wrong
till there's no voice left in me to sing,
no more songs to Thee to be sung.

COME LIVE ALONE WITH ME

Whitman feels it burning in him,
the sap rising, grapes fermenting.
He'll teach us how to dance.
Look for him under our boot-soles,
he says.

Or listen well to Mr. Keats: his ode
where two young lovers' urgencies
are always just about to crest.
Come on! Have not we done
the love-fade mishap half to death!

If less is more, try something less
this time — be wife and husband
summers only, mow the grass,
clean the basement, feed the cats,
make love, mow the lawn again.

First signs of fall, unplug the clock.

THAT SORT OF THING

At the bachelor bash for my friend,
a girl jumps out of the cake
and I end up driving her home.

She's a religion major at the college.
The stag parties pay the tuition.
In our attempts at serious talk

while licking frosting off her lips,
we exchange numbers and interests,
our love of nature, that sort of thing.

A few nights after, we're camping
in Cathedral Park in West Virginia,
lying on our backs, holding hands,

talking up the writers we know best.
She can quote Emerson by heart:
If the stars should appear

but once in every thousand years,
how man would believe and adore.
I'm more than a little impressed.

In the tent, I break out the butter
and Irish cream. You know the rest.
First light of day, she's off to class.

Another thousand years to wait.

THEREFORE

Hades doesn't think, therefore he does.
He whisks her into his underground den,
youth for his age, a little love, why not.

But six months on the throne of death
is all she can stand to sit at one stretch.
She begs him to see her needs for once,

for the love of the gods and mama above,
to return her to her spring-making gifts
from which she's been unkindly cut.

Now Hades begins to think, dear Zeus,
I'm fucked! I've forgotten how to sleep alone.
The warmth down here is no longer enough.

THE LITTLE FLAME

Because we like pretending,
I lash her slender wrists
to the thick upper bed posts,
and her feet to the bottom.

Her boyfriend is watching
from his photo on the dresser.
And when she begs, please sir,
I let the ropes go one by one.

Then once we've had our fill
of silly fun, we sit like yogis
on the carpet, light the candle
in the bottle in between us.

From her side of the flame,
she sees me as an old lame dog
whose eyes say put me down.
I see in her the gun and bullet.

The little flame, it flickers on.

PLAYING TIME

Look at Jesus, who tells
adulteresses whom he loves
to go and sin no more.
Or Joseph, who won't succumb
to the pretty wife of Potiphar.
They're the ones on God's first team.

But Sampson, Adam, and that lot,
who lose their power to women —
second stringers, water boys.

D. H. Lawrence got it right.
You want a deeper bond?
Stand up to one another.

You want some playing time
on next year's squad?
Then get into God's line of sight.
Stand up an inch or two taller.

THE REPTILIAN PART

The end begins as a shiver,
a flutter, a twitch, a summer cold,
a bump on a tire, a silent stroke
in the reptilian brain.

It's almost nothing to notice,
but still I sleep poorly,
wake up edgy and confused,
make love with my eyes closed,
pretending you're someone
I don't know.

In the den, I watch reruns
and lose myself in solitaire,
snapping the cards on the table,
king on the ace, queen on the king,
jack, ten, nine, eight, ad nauseam . . .

LYING ALONE WITH YOU

So. Look at us. No longer one,
grasping for the other in our sleep,
unable to make the loose ends meet.

Of course he didn't steal you quite,
beyond one night or two. Can two
(or maybe three) short trysts compete

with years and years of honesty,
predictable tomorrows?
It's ridiculous to think it. Yet,

for the ancients, the snake was like
an immortal god who slithers
out of last year's skin.

And here's my newest sorrow:
how dry and wrinkled honesty becomes
against a few short hours of pleasure.

PART II

LOW NOON

THE MASSACRE

Dad dug their grave behind the barn,
then loaded up his thirty-aught-six
to shoot a bunch of feral cats.
If I understood him right,
they'd overrun the farm.

Who'll catch the mice, I asked.
He wasn't much for explaining.
Jesus didn't die on the cross
for every kitty to run wild,
I'd heard him say to Mom.

That morning something ended.
It made me dizzy watching Dad
scoop broken bodies off the grass
by the tail or the scruff of the neck
and toss them yowling into the pit.

Was he going to bury Puss alive!
What relief to hear the pounding tip
of his spade finish up our unkind task,
then silence, crickets singing,
the spade at rest.

Oh, I played my part just fine,
and have acted it well ever since,
pretending I like being part of this
outside work that's asked of a man.
And if I remember correctly,

what a lucky son I thought I was
to have a father who included me
in pitiless jobs that had to be done,
and a mom who stayed in the house
with my sisters.

WE DO THE BEST WITH WHAT WE'VE GOT

Beneath the falls, at last alone
in a cloister of smoking stumps,
we'll kiss and talk in tongues
like newborn born-agains.

Are we lost or found? she'll ask.

How can we be lost, I'll laugh,
if He is everywhere.

He's watching us, she'll say next.
He likes to watch, I'll be thinking.

Don't touch me there, she'll gasp,
but words won't matter much by then.
We've called it desire since heaven
knows when, and once the tip's in
very few of us can stop.

We'll scrabble up the bluff
and quench our mutual thirst
and then we'll talk about it.
She'll say the world is clean
if seen from far enough above.
I'll tell her of my recent dream
where she's a mare hot for Jesus,
I'm a mule with a fair-sized penis
(we do the best with what we've got),
and Father's somewhere up there
watching. Relaxed. Refreshed.
Very happy with us.

RECONNOITERING WITH THE SOLDIER WITHIN

Eventually the woman happens along
who snubs you for someone more sane.
"Less volatile" is how she explains it.

But it doesn't bend you out of shape.
He's not the man you are, you think,
and who understands personal taste.

Plus on the whole you're quite content
to sleep alone. No great difference,
sleeping alone or holding someone else.

Different pressures. Different dreams.
For a while, of course, there's the pain,
and those wretched self-help books

that she left behind for you to find,
now face-down across your bed
like rows of flattened army tents.

LOW NOON

Months after I knew it was over,
since we last kissed, or had a talk
long enough to be nuanced,

there comes a second kind of silence.
Drizzly cold, say, twelve o'clock,
could be today, November tenth,

the phone doesn't ring, the postman
doesn't bring the unexpected letter.
I half forget to check the box.

The trees have dropped their leaves.
The noon sun barely tops the trees.
I'm not thinking of her either.

REFRAIN

So many graves to fill/ Oh love aren't you tired yet.

Don't ask to visit, please.
I live in a different house now.
You don't know my new address,
nor should you try to find it out.

Don't phone, don't sing me songs.
If you feel the need to correspond,
suppress yourself, or meditate
on Leonard Cohen's "The Faith."

The refrain is what I'm thinking of.
Sit on the mat, with your back straight,
legs crossed; reflect on love as longing
for a good and long night's sleep.

Don't think of us as failed or sad.
As love drops down into its grave,
finally deep enough,
imagine us as brave at last.

JIMS

Jims like me wake up in life
already playing second fiddle
in realms of sex and love —
indistinct, undistinguished,
thousands of us hungering
for never offered solo parts.

Nans like her float among us,
plain as sin, but soft for Jims
and singing hopeful hymns
to God and Jesus.

Across the aisle, Clarences,
eyes too big, are sweet on Nans.
Their brand new homely hearts
are bleeding down their sleeves,
while in-betweens like Jims are
bleating for fiery-eyed sopranos
in front row center seats.

Jims lift weights, eat right, stay trim,
play bridge and chess with Clarences,
jog barefoot on the beach alone,
do not disturb the universe.

They think they'll leave the Nans behind,
but end up Nan men down the line.

DENTS

Dad buys a good used truck,
changes the oil and sparkplugs
himself, keeps it nice and spiffy.
Something breaks, he fixes it.
A dent, he bumps it out.

So, naturally, my father's son,
when I fall asleep in my van
in the Last Call parking lot,
I wish it didn't have this gash
in the front where I hit the tree.
I'd rather crash in a perfect van,
a van Dad would be proud of.

Mom's dad, Grandpa Cleve,
he'd let his pick-up go to hell,
and then he'd buy a new one.
He was another kind of man.
Showed me how to loosen up.
He couldn't read a lick of music,
but he could make a fiddle sing.
Mom said he'd have half the bar
dancing to the Texas Shuffle.

The day I saw him in his coffin,
I asked Mom if I could touch him,
and did, till Dad said that's enough.

Enough for him he must have meant.

BORN ONCE

For several days we barely slept.
She stretched out her arms for me
to lie with her in summer's grass.
Across the creek a revival meeting
was gaining momentum, old time
religion in an outdoor pavilion.

Above the altar, *Ye Must*
Be Born Again was written big.
Dear God, she said, be born once first!
She was tired of summer flings.

My dad, a church-going man,
warned me how on chilly nights,
I'd want me a wife — with some luck
a superior woman worth cuddling with.
And by late September, there she was,
revealing something new every day,
hitching up her dress, flashing me
a shapely thigh, half complaining
that her former lovers hadn't
cherished her enough.

BARELY KISSING, THEN ALL THIS

Our lips were scarcely touching.
I breathed out, she breathed me in.
She knew I had a wife, sort of.
We just made love, she said.

At first, I barely comprehended
how naturally she held my hand,
what's more, how much I liked it.
But driving back to Cumberland,

I saw the night as strangely near,
with giant stars like children draw.
Hugging the shoulder of the road,
I steered by Saturn's moons

and broken middle lines on Mars.
Common things, like signs and cars,
I had no words to know them by.
When I got home, I wasn't there.

A YEARNING

All the men in her head
made me jealous and sad.
"It's me or them," I said.
She married me instead.
She liked to fuck with me
no doubt. I wondered.

We wrote our own vows.
I promised to stop saying
I love you all the while,
and she promised to start
thinking less about them
and more like a wife.

We walked this new hope
for us to the top of a hill
overlooking a graveyard
in the shape of a heart.
I yearned to be buried
in there with her one day.

But we had just agreed
to spend more time apart.

PART III

PUTTING MY BODY TO BED

UNASKED

Be ye therefore perfect

This or that improves over time.
Poetry: I make smarter tropes.
Tennis: I master new shots,

a top-spin lob, a forehand slice.
Sex: I learn to slow it down.
But can I teach myself to love?

I can always lose a pound or two,
buy new shoes to make me taller.
But how tall is tall enough

to learn to turn the other cheek,
or forgive her back to me in bed,
or wash the cellar steps unasked?

POWER LINES

I haven't always felt like this, but
the crooked tooth in your otherwise
pretty mouth bothers me to no end.

And your ears a mite large, sticking out,
my eyes go straight to them, and linger
for a while. Same ears I once adored.

It didn't happen overnight, but I feel
stronger when I focus — though I hide it —
on what's wrong with you. The faults

in your countenance too, like that anger
you're always trying to hide from me,
off to the corner of your smile.

It's like we were a pristine mountain
that has been gouged for power lines,
a tiny brown strip

compared to the whole wide green of it.
But now when I look at that mountain,
the gouge is what I see.

AT THE HALLOWEEN BALL

I'm dressed up like a slut,
four inch high heels, high cut
blouse to hide my hairy chest.
A Marilyn mole on my cheek.

It takes a real man, so I'm told,
to see the woman underneath.
I take a hit of Acapulco gold,
and gaze in the glass unafraid.

As the party clicks along, I strut
and flirt and have so much fun
that even Christ and Magdalene
can't conceive who I really am,

while all of them are obvious,
including him across the room,
the thug, one hand on his dick,
the other resting on his gun.

CUTTING OFF THE INNER WOMAN

My inner woman came out of the closet
dressed to kill, wearing a low-cut blouse,

hot to play poker, or happy to watch —
the perfect match I'd always wanted.

We found our stride at the racetrack,
an easy rhythm right out of the gate.

But the second furlong was a disaster —
unpleasant words exchanged with Mom,

bankbook exhausted, credit cards maxed.
A kick, a buck, a slap, a bite,

the second place, the photo-finish,
when we had put it all on winning,

then postmortems that lasted past dinner.
No blackjack tonight, no yum yum, nothing.

And hand me, please, that tin of aspirin.
I feel a migraine coming on.

YOU HEAR A FLY FART WHEN YOU DIE

Your first thought when You feel your heart
on fire is — to Shove a Flick into the VCR.
Anything but This — the dying part — You
don't think about It, don't give It Power.

You mop the kitchen Floor instead, and wax
your Truck and car. Maybe you are feeling
better — a little tightness in the Ribs. God
only knows Where — the little Woman is

on days you spend Apart, no questions asked.
No need to Panic yet. You read a magazine
on how to Drop ten pounds of fat — and Not
be hungry. All else Failing, you try praying,

but unprepared to pray in Blood and sweat,
you Shriek instead — "dear God, oh Shit!"
And that is when there intervenes the Fly.
Then you Die and you've been dead since.

ONE LESS

Not a word from her in days.
I play a game of computer
chess and lose, then rummage
through the fridge for lunch,

half hearing the bell, but not
even asking for whom . . .
Good riddance. One her less.
All the more grub for myself.

I'm an educated man with lots
of noble thoughts.
How dare she call me a thug.

DUSK IN PARANOIA

After our game of cribbage,
we have a short conversation
on love and truth, that religious shit.

A-fucking-men. I'm starting to get it.
She talks to you about me some.

Then I go home and sit near the phone,
small chance in hell to ring from her again,
unless to rub it in: we're through, kaput.

Spot on. It would be the truest thing
she ever said.

Nightfall, capital N.
On the porch swing, I smoke myself numb.
This cacophony of screech owls and bull frogs
is a poor excuse for a hymn.

I feel like loading up the 12-gauge
and making something dead.

INCARNATE

Mission accomplished.

Think of me as family farm help,
working off my low self-esteem,
hell-bent to erase all doubts of my worth.

Imagine me messing with our sacred cow,
suddenly on fire for her reputed big heart,
her lost deep eyes, her heifer-perfect twat.

See me as four feet tall, with an eight inch cock,
standing on a large rock, deflowering Americud,
so to speak, though this is not her first rodeo,
mounted by a puffed-up runt like me.

VENGENCE IS MINE

If silence wasn't the better move now,
I'd smash this deadbolt off my tongue

and drown you in a flood of venom,
a lightning storm of hate-slash-love;

address you as your royal hind-end,
pronounce your wanderlust as scum;

declare to you my own deep hunger
to pay you back my pain redoubled,

while on both knees, you beg of me
for one last chance to prove me wrong —

at which point I'd feign forgiveness,
as if I knew not what you'd done.

THE DIRT ON US

Darkness becomes me.
My skin is cancer-pocked.
I gimp along on my last legs
while you're still strong,
well hinged.

You're headed east.
I'm staying home.
That's best for both of us.
Where you'll see rising suns,
blameless babies being born,
I'd see a die-off coming on —
enlightened hospices,
opiate dispensaries,
pain free deaths,
heated coffins.

No big whoop if people talk.
We walked the same path
for as far as it went.

Here's to the dirt on us.
You think you'll love again;
I dream and walk in half-worlds
under the stars and black holes
where thinking takes a breath.

I'm falling out of love with thought.
Almost nothing really hurts.

BODY DAYS

Undone, replaced, half lost,
stumbling into the kitchen
to brew coffee, eight o'clock,
sleep reading the news on line,
sleep driving the van to work,

I'm practicing my life
without a body.

The one I had is gone.
My lover has left it for dead.
In body days, erogenous days,
you'd find us in the mornings,
fresh from sex, in coffee shops,

with heavy cream dripping
from our mugs.

Now at Starbucks, Second Cup,
Daily Grind, a placid grace —
a second sleep — is coming on.
I'm laying down my storybook,
turning me over onto my back,

putting baby, my body, to bed,
careful not to wake him up.

A SPARROW IN THE HOUSE

I'm napping in front of the tube
when you show up, like an omen,
like a dream, swooping from room
to room, landing in my potted tree.
You try to hide yourself within
the leaves, but don't succeed.

Your eyes lock into mine.
You chill me, feathered friend.
We're as close as birth and breath,
and yet as far apart as two things
born from eggs can stretch.

I can think, but you,
birdbrain, can fly.

So fly. Be gone. Be free.
Here's an open door, now shoo.
God's eyes may well be on you, too,
but you don't belong in my house.
If that means killing you, I will.

Law and Order's coming on.
It's way too late for us.

PART IV

LORD MAKE ME CHASTE,
BUT NOT YET

CLAIRVOYANT

Before I am Jim I am
some kind of criminal,
Nancy says, seeping
down into her trance.
I'm supposed to take notes.

A man is flying to Vegas
and out of the blue his head
is thrust back against the seat.
He sees two propellers burning,
earth coming up to greet him,
little houses growing bigger —
here Nancy screams.

She's working very hard,
I write on my yellow pad.

A silence. A dramatic sigh.
An Irish or a Scottish lad, a boy
and his sister, no parents, she says,
are crossing the sea to America,
the ship breaking up in a storm.
Nancy's sobbing now.

She's earning her money, I write.
I have Scottish roots. I'm tight.
I'm afraid of water over my head.
Nancy's on to me.

A hooded man in time arrives.
My hands are tied behind my back.

I'm praying for an experienced
hangman, someone who knows
where to put the knot.

Underneath, a trap door drops
to start my journey down.

Nancy seems quite out of breath.

THINKING OVER LOVE

I admire the cardinals,
their colors, the crimson male,
the female's subtle tints of red
around her beak and tail.

Their fidelity. It opens up
an ancient ache inside my heart,
the alerts they sing to each other
if I'm outside making them edgy.
It seems so right at dusk, tonight,
these wild birds, yoked for life,
fortifying their nest for winter.

Or maybe not. Jesus, for what
I know, they could be building
separate winter nests this fall,
giving each other a little space,
taking time apart, flying solo
for a while, seeing who they are
alone, perchance. Good luck.

If I talked bird, I'd speak up.
Life's one hell of a stretch
to wing it all by yourself.

But then again, what's more
alone than two becoming one.

LUCKY TAO QUIN

I'm tired of fretting about stuff
like keeping up with the Smiths.
And should I be tempted again,
I'll meditate on Tao Quin
in ancient China.

For food he fished and tended
his garden, or just went hungry.
Mortgage his soul to his guts?
He'd done that once in a city,
working at a desk.

But never again, he promised.
After his house burned down,
the stars were now his ceiling.
Nothing was lost. If it rained,
he slept under his boat.

If he had it, he loved good wine,
shared it with friends, then read
poems they had written together,
played the zither, contemplated
the shortness of a life.

In his own good time, he rebuilt.
The neighbors showed up to help,
bearing gifts. The girls walked by
and peeked in. Skinny Tao Quin.
The sexiest Buddha ever.

THE RENUNCIATE

Her idea of a good time was us,
alone in a small room with a desk,
reading *The Bhagavad Gita.*

Her idea of a good breakfast
was oatmeal and sesame seeds.
As I was poor, that worked for me.

Her favorite prayer was silence,
or writing in her spiritual diary.
I wasn't big on talking either.

Lunch was nuts, a slice of cheese.
I was drawn to her stringency
in everything. Except for sex.

The dot on her head turned me on,
and when she chanted Hare Krishna,
she sounded like a goddess.

Her goal was to see the world anew.
Her practice was my window view:
a used car lot and a parking garage.

If she saw it afresh, as a god unmasked,
she'd hitch up her dress and sit on my lap,
then I could see more clearly, too.

THE YEAR GOD AND I BECAME ONE

If I make my bed in hell, behold, thou art there.

That year I rarely strayed
from my routine. Weekdays,
odd-jobbing to pay the rent;
nights, reading horror fiction,
and sometimes the Bible,
to keep myself sane.

Winter was frigid, depressing,
but come spring, I did my best
to feel better. Weather permitting
I'd lie down in green pastures.
The pear trees had blossomed,
the blue-bells were out.

It was my year of living simply,
with nobody else in the house.
God and I were washing the dishes,
God and I were brushing our teeth,
God and I were crawling into bed,
God and I were feeling listless,
half bored with one another.

But then it'd be morning again.
The air was perfumed with lilac.
The asparagus was popping up
amongst the weeds and flowers.
We'd start the day on our knees,
as if we had one set between us,
one neck to wear the holy beads
that June had forgotten to pack
when she'd left all in a huff.

I liked that His son mentioned
the importance of daily bread
along with all the bigger stuff,
like hallowed kingdoms, debt
relief, enemy forgiveness.

I changed one line, however.
There wasn't much evil going on
in our little neck of the woods.
I'd know evil when I saw it.
Deliver us, I said, from ego.

By the dog days of August,
the mail wasn't worth checking.
Wasn't worth the walk to the box.
The letter from June wasn't coming.
I'd stopped reading, quit my jobs.
The phone almost never rang,
and when it did, I let God get it.

Hell was time and we were in it.
By fall we didn't even talk.

THE PROPOSAL

We live together separately,
buy a duplex; his and her sides,
separate entrances and keys.

Think of the long-term savings.
One mortgage. One lawn to mow.
One mower. One tank of gas.

And the convenience. If I broke
my fist against the wall again,
you could drive me to the doctor.
Or when your gynecology report
came in with question marks,
or if your daughter or a friend
said you were looking old today,
I could be Johnny on the spot,
sweep you up into my arms,
and say it just ain't so.

We'd have off days, no doubt,
but if you played a horrid round
of golf, you know I'd be willing,
even if reluctantly, to talk about it.
Were you fully rotating your hips?
Keeping your eye on the ball?

Or take that book I'm writing —
if I got a case of writer's block,
or the plot wasn't taking shape,
on nights my door wasn't locked,
you'd pop in and help me out.

We all face death alone,
but when it came my time to go,
you'd be by my side, as close
as beings get this side of heaven,
whispering *je t'aime* and all that.

Nor would I have to fly to Quebec
for your last rites. It's a definite
win win situation.

LAST TANGO UP SHIT CREEK

Here she is, sitting on her deck,
rolling her hair up in a bun,
We're both an hour late for work.

Just before I took that shot,
I remember horsing around,
undoing her blouse
she had just buttoned up.
She saw a blue herring
rising out of the morning mist
hanging over Evitts Creek.

Up-Shit Creek, she called it,
where she lives. I didn't know
her humor yet.

Look, she whispered,
That's a blue heron.
That's a sign.

That we're in love? I asked.

Our good-bye kiss went on too long
and we decided to call in sick.
Love sick, I suggested.
What's the rush, she said.
We laughed.

Back inside the still warm bed,
I cupped again the curve of her hips,
the arch of her back, her perfect breasts,
everything yes, her hands on my chest,

the scars on one wrist, up and down.
How you do it if you're serious.

Sweetheart, I gasped. What's this?
She put her hand over my mouth.
"Last Tango" comes to mind now,
when Brando covers Maria's lips
as she's about to say her name.
No names! he shouts!
No pasts, he means.

The story I remember best
(if only it had stopped with that)
is her strung-out mother sneaking
her a ticket for the Greyhound bus
to help her run away from her dad,
and then forgetting to meet her
at the station. She was six.

My god, she could have been
one of those *missing children* pics
they used to put on grocery sacks
before they switched to plastic bags.

It only made me love her more.
I swear to God that's how I felt.
But once that talk door opened,
the talk went on too long.

Here she's dressed for work again,
and we're back on the front deck.
She's not talking now, except
one time to scream in my face
to put the fuckin' camera down.

Four deer in a line — one buck,
three does — cleared a distant fence.
But we didn't say jack shit again.
The morning mist was gone.
The sun had burned it off.

I was back inside my truck
when a hawk swooped down,
flashing its red tail, snatching
a rabbit out of the weeds,
within a giant's grasp
of my driver's window.
It balanced on the wind
like a first prize photograph,
then glided up shit creek
to somewhere more private
for dinner.

DEATH IN APRIL

I'm raking last year's leaves,
feeling how empty and weak
my arms have become.

The all-of-a-sudden April sun
has blossomed the meadows
with wild yellow mustard.

The daffodils are bursting
into flower and next will come
the irises, peonies, on and on.

April's got her Sphinx-like eye
on men like me — lackluster,
falling down on the job.

Not that I'm ready to die quite yet.
Just a bit tired of hanging around.

THE REHAB BLUES

Autumnwood. Old age
wasted on the elderly.
I'm just visiting, I think.
I'm half way out the door,
but Nurse Ratched spies me
on my walker and wrestles
my sorry ass back to 103
by the ear, so to speak.

I test her lips for a crack
in the ice, a flicker of fun.
Take your meds, she barks,
then straps me into the bed.
She'll untie me when I start
behaving right, she snaps.

I've always had a soft spot
for haughty pretty women.

At four a.m. the percoset,
laxative and aceteminophin
are kicking in and I'm a mess.
The wall becomes the floor.
The ceiling's now the wall.
Nurse R undoes my straps
and whacks me in the nuts,
as if to say WAKE UP!,
then waltzes down the hall.

READING WHITMAN AT DUSK

When I was wild and young,
before I knew a poem existed,
I thought the rising sun was one;
and the mountains blooming
in redbud and dogwood,
and the everyday rivers
I waded and fished in.

Now the river's fished out,
the mountain's been stripped
for power and whatnots,
yachts for the strippers;
and for the common man,
all kinds of stuff, air miles,
pain pills, antidepressants,
riding tractors, wall-sized
televisions, knee and hip
replacements.

I'm on the doctor's waiting list.

In this unbending night,
are you still there, Whitman,
in perfect health, untamed,
under my boot-soles, happy
to greet me?

All I see is dust and dirt.

That said, and understood,
my nights are fine, dear poet.
And dawns aren't half bad either.
Twilights. Dusks. The in-betweens.

The light of day is when it hurts.

HOSPICE

I descend the golden steps
to the rocky ledge of Lethe Creek.
I stick my big toe in. That's it.

Since nothing's new under the sun,
a tiny death could be just the ticket,
like a two-week winter vacation.

And one big toe is all it takes.
Something starts to smell good,
and here she comes, my appetite,
like some higher form of clockwork,
her slow swaying hips, her pointy,
higher kind of tits, playing nurse,
seeking out my hiding place.

She's bringing in my supper,
fish and mashed potatoes.

You're different, she says,
bending down to please me.

CARRYING WATER, CHOPPING WOOD

Mop the living room floor,
move the furniture around,
feed the cat, water the plant,
shake out the long hall rug,
lay it in the yard to sun,
and don't forget to think.

Read a page of sacred text.
Give it some time to sink in.
A hint of truth is like a seed
of winter wheat germinating
in the snow. Think deeply,
and as slowly as you can.

Reflect on someone gone,
whoever pops into your head.
Your grandma. An ex-wife.
A friend who died in youth.
See birth and death as in
and out, one more, one less,

like breathing. Pay the bills,
wash the truck, mow the grass.
Take a bath, brush your teeth.
Call the kids to say goodnight.
You've made your bed.
Go lie in it.

LORD MAKE ME CHASTE, BUT NOT YET

Imitating the life of Christ,
I'd like to have a few free days
after I die to embrace my wise
and cloven-footed side.

Hell is all that I expected anyway.
Theatre, art, deep conversation,
ass kicking sex, no holds barred,
just enough pain to call it pleasure.
Orgasms that last for ten minutes
for men and women alike.

Or that's how I'll explain myself
cross-dressed up in heaven,
should I arrive a little late.

NOTES

The epigraph for "Refrain" — page 21 — is from Leonard Cohen's "The Faith."

The epigraph for "Unasked" — page 28 — is from *The New Testament*, "Matthew" 5:48.

The epigraph for "Incarnate" — page 35 — is a quote from George W. Bush.

The epigraph for "The Year God and I Became One" — page 45 — is from *The Old Testament*, "Psalms," 139:8.

ABOUT THE AUTHOR

James (Jim) Ralston lives on three and a half acres between Rocky Gap Creek and Evitts Creek outside of Cumberland, Maryland, a post-industrial town still trying to find its way forward. This land and this Appalachian town are the settings for most of the *Lyrics for a Low Noon*.

Ralston teaches English and Theatre at Blue Ridge Technical and Community College, Martinsburg, West Virginia. He has also taught at Shepherd University (Shepherdstown, WV), Frostburg State University (Frostburg, MD), and Central Michigan University (Mt. Pleasant, Michigan), with a few other short stops along the way.

His publications include *The Choice of Emptiness*, a series of essays that also works as a novel; *The Appalachian Grammar Shop*; and, over a span of 35 years, numerous essays and poems in *The Sun: A Magazine of Ideas*. As well, his work has appeared in various other journals and newspapers, including the *Utne Reader* and the *Pittsburgh Post-Gazette*. For fifteen years, between 1990 and 2005, he was a regular columnist for the *Charleston Gazette*, West Virginia's state paper.

He has written four plays, acted in some of them, directed some of them, most recently "35 Folds to the Moon" at the New Embassy Theatre in Cumberland and the Apollo Theatre in Martinsburg.

Presently Ralston writes a monthly blog, which can be found at jameslralston.com.

www.ingramcontent.com/pod-product-compliance
Lightning Source LLC
Chambersburg PA
CBHW032030090426

42741CB00006B/799